Jaguar Harmonics :

Person Woven of Tesserae

Library of Congress Cataloging-in-Publication Data

Waldman, Anne, 1945- author.
  [Poems. Selections]
  Jaguar Harmonics : Person Woven of Tesserae / Anne Waldman.
    pages cm
  ISBN 978-0-942996-81-4
  I. Title.
  PS3573.A4215A6 2014
  811'.54—dc23

                            2014001197

Thanks to Alystyre Julian, Simone Fattal, Etel Adnan, Jerome Rothenberg,
Anselm Berrigan, and *The Brooklyn Rail.*

The Post-Apollo Press
35 Marie Street
Sausalito, California 94965
www.postapollopress.com

Book Design by Simone Fattal
Cover drawing & interior design elements by Etel Adnan
Typeset by Lindsey Boldt in Bell MT text
with Trajan & Tw Cen MT display

Printed in the United States of America on acid-free paper

Jaguar Harmonics :

Person Woven of Tesserae

ANNE WALDMAN

THE POST-APOLLO PRESS

ALSO BY ANNE WALDMAN :

for Susan Manchester
- guardian -

"A place where all the unknown past and the emergent future meet in a vibrating soundless hum."

— William S. Burroughs

"This is not my story to tell.

Jaguars were always the keepers of the jungle—lumen-eyed-cosmic-cats, strong bodied and wild. The people of the Amazon held immense respect for these creatures. They wanted to learn from them. They wanted to know more. The hunters would track the Jaguars, noting their hunting abilities and approaches from a distance. They found that when not hunting, the Jaguar would meander through the Jungle in search of a vine; once the wild cat had found what it was looking for, it would eat the vine, purge and sprawl out spread-eagle on the Jungle floor for hours, eyes wide seeing beyond the canopy; beyond the galaxy. The hunters
witnessed this and wondered just what was happening to the great hunter of the forest, now docile and silent. They gathered the vine and took it with them.

This is how Yagé was discovered.

This is how Jaguars came to be known as the keepers of the Cosmos."

— Angel Dominguez

of tinsel?
  you want to say insulated
nary scold a child-woman made of
  of what? of person!
nay nay go down all a hook of lumen
 makes "of" and "woven of" seem light
person…and person what do you know of light?
 of your meme of: tour of an ordinary wild-mind person
and person as journeyman-woman?
is not a tree meme exactly but a state of jungle?
  of long forest occurring over time,
not as Cambrian but as child as contemporary person
  blink your eye it's archaic person as person
is liana is not machete
  but ornament in complexity
is grit of the multitudinous mental universes
as real as person's poems?
and
is softer person now because she imbibed her own light?

come below borders of all you imagine
O my persons

as if you were coming up through inchoative eons to mental talk

crept across Beringia

a Person woven of psychotropic-shards, fur and bone

a Person woven of glimmer, of cure

clicks of Xhosa

a Person woven of malachite ritual
where pestles grind the vine

unearth the green, click of stone

command passes over a Persian motif
stalk and ambush
who crosses Tezcatlipoca

Puntumayo the source
condor flight
long lay low longs to sink down here prowl
    mud knee high longing jaguar lope
if you were summoned winging   fly low
    would believe you?
your mental wingspan

if you were listening and spoken to in neutral speech
     would believe you?
who rules in the night-top of the food chain
would...
would believe you?

 condor holds a snake in volcanic vision statuary
     St. Augustin

& the cat talks to you in her crepuscular power-mode
mind-to-mind

how far back does a seer go
& in what form
43,000 BCE?

sea elf offers elixir for long life

jade medicine cup sits in the museum in Ecuador 5,000 years old

Person woven of sound bands   bells   rattles

Person woven of multiple mammal bands you try on, around many
     waists
a one of them, ominous and lumbering approaches the
                              glint-rise of drawn-out–dawn
another: you are a nursing mother in never ended aubade
waiting with your species to arise

red cord around your waist with knots for blood time

armed and waiting, psyche intact to be milked

down the grind
　　elemental–metal problem don't kill it

Person woven of vulnerability don't kill it

so that the ecosphere takes notice
miles underground of itself on top of you
ektos—outside,　　Plasma—that which has form
ectoplasm (the paranormal)

what tries to tell us of mammal stealth
active filaments
unprecedented warnings with consonants of "H" and "W"
& hissing sounds and groan　*heh heh heh*

& I'll say it again the suffering on this land
palpable right under you
what done to the *indigenes*
rip and torture of their person
emasculation
& to the land
& to the science
& to the medicine
& to the children
the whole genocide
what summoning to tell you this? *heh heh*

brain a storehouse of gigantic suffering
go nine years into darkness

don't like it don't do it don't like it don't do it
hydraulic fracturing *heh heh*
shattering under you don't don't do it
Person woven of performing sutras don't don't
the thunder said don't do it and symmetry said *heh heh*

and gambols to the flight of the asteroid

Person woven of nimble words, mere fractions of them
ag and *ar* and *ra* as antidote to gloom

woven of white poppy *gar ra ra tsa ma ma*

whist whist whist heh heh

of the power of the centaur's heel woven by a poet
in the sky above you

Person woven of spheres enclosing spheres

Person woven of Morse code of digitizing "distance now"

And gambols to the flight of the asteroid

trajectory think "distance now"

and of the nimbus of a swerve
as if it could move light years
already happened   but not yet
did it "lightyear" a gap?

bioluminescence
slowed down the tinsel neon

with Moses in the bulrushes

who believe and summon here?

can't drink your descriptive power

over the cupmouth I rise

a candle, an orange Halloween bucket with a happy face

who would glower when you get too tight

Person woven "too fast"

rapido   muy rapido

they said of her: still could burn

tightened up too fast, too hard, too fast and still moving

Person woven from what hovers at the doorway

pawing at the ground
Person woven mundane

Person woven like monkey kinetics
or too cocksure

fond and tentative or back at the doorway lurches forward or back

would go wouldn't go then would then wouldn't
whist whist whist

who believe you in your lab coat *whist whist* small guinea pigs
your precision instrument needs greater testing and probe

Person woven of solving and not-solving
and pressure of a bounce through a threshold to celebrate decibels
Kundry disappears into the undergrowth

roots up   to   pull your psyche   down under
   dirt and leaves...
sorceress cursed of no centuries rest...

accretion's musical memory
   earliest was cycladic rhythm her timing her measure
insulin wars

Huguenot ancestry mystery
   or mastery of survival coded

will you run, swim, dive across a lifetime of persecution

female of all females would run
   swim and breathe across the boundary hounded hooded
     persecution

Person woven of forest time and running

Person woven of savannah metrics

Person born of a violinist who played and died way before the

strings grew thin and weak

Person with one thousand four hundred cubic centimeter brain

entopic brain, gestation of pliant harmonics

in the place within place that is pre-recorded desire

O Asia! a cheetah–like–sunny–housecat–in–her–stripes
    would pounce upon

edenic brain, inebriant one

sun sun sun sun sun sun sun sun

Person woven of monoliths may be mere glass

Person of a mirage that would be fate of all ancestor scrys

Person that is the core of galaxy she seizes

our Milky path, a poetics of influence

bricolage of sensibility made for future fur bits

Person woven of monoliths still standing but fall down

proprietary then modest
clean up messes the body makes mockery of

and you can't just go around killing and conquering persons
you can't just take them out at midnight and rape and slaughter
and kill persons

build it, Pleiades said

feeling alone I — I — I — he was wasn't singing your vision
dreaming alone person alone, curandero wasn't singing your vision in
Pleiades wasn't singing it in I — I — I
sending it in *aye-aye-aye*

Curandero sing it in call upon you Pleiades sing it in

you alone sitting and crumbled, crumpled? *aye aye*
& what is best for this and into the crystal mirror
into the sky
see yourself, repent?

and what is best you lie down and sink down to send it in
and send your crystal casket into rhythms of outer space
embrace a 3–brane world

lucid inside
and your "remains" watching and looking
your remains when you have been burnt out
and nurtured to burn out
watching and looking still lucid at the fire pit
you are cinder

center of the universe

Person woven of chronometers

Person a chip so small

or ember growing to size of Saturn
Person woven of flames of tension

jaded, see the souvenir of person

a little chain over her head

a utility object

opener, a key, a reminder

Snakey markings on vines intricate
as markings of the tortoise oracle

who summon & who believe?

Person Quick-to-See

Person Slower-in-Step

asp of hope, serpent's aspiration, "mental" it? *heh heh heh*

cool down, a sorcerer's misery
cool down the trance and truth serum
of unsolved Jerusalem
   injured
in truth
as if the world can't face truth
human a bond of the bestial

ferocious
   flaws

claws......elongated claws
   against the face, of yours and yours
& printed cleft festered
the back of my neck
I carry all these Persons inside who walk my spine
digress with small carnivores
rhythm's broken vertebrae

Person woven of pivots

a con of ego in flaws of endtime

madre says You old gal!

you old old gal!

matters, all snag a *madre*
    just as a circle remains *madre su madre*

        gaunt gal with broken held–together–vertebra
shuffle in the dance line

    and matters arrive again & meow money
    Tell em my Paris, my Mexico, my mid East
Colombia I thirsted for
of family
roots broken
blood poured out of my eyes

I see your blood too come out of you, earth eyes

People reason science too many for the plantation
O scene's & geography's a hold history for

what we made strife of

for others

Person woven of cruelty

and then again, of cruelty
said the Jaguar
of nothing yet you've seen this earth

author of false thins eject

I a poor somber eye

race for it
mode as

ever sore a gravid one in thinning things

And the elder poet came of Lebanon and said

we're all in debt to one's wonder,
*   signals of the medicine world*
come down to the same root word or caesura,
*   to the comma and the littler increments and we will*
be the seeds they are, and be the green ornaments they are
*   and please to magic and please please to magic come…*

Person woven of trace elements and scent of Lebanon

that migrates what she knows through the book world

and will not hold off
and will not let go

and loves her night sky patterning down

quitter curst

said it's because of blunt instruments

I said, said, saying
I quitter said I
a quiet

a new tower quits of itself, no coin

desert the color of which is anger

No No I said to them (the voices's echoes)

it is a neutral face

Person of cosmetics walk away

Person of responsibility walk away
how be summoned

& who to respond?

Never quit responding

which is
of lute, divine
sense roots
diverse habit
women, of many animals fur and claw
orgy of skin, interdictions
then cry your preview's legible doubt

Person woven of doubt

limpid alarm
Dr. Lazarus is best

when all the best intentioned die down at night

lie down and sleep

it will be the century no longer yours

take my word, Person woven of words

photon! listen, photon!

jolt of space-time travel
how elemental you are
hiding your substructure

it will be up to the keepers of the future we imprint upon
now? arise?

go, now?

where fermions where quarks where leptons where bosons
and the bison went down

more than ever the rich doth hate the public

although Richness talks with a smooth velvety voice

quaint no more, richness, thy name is Devil

dissipate money

& boasts are to a limit

escutcheon a surrogate name
for riches are nutrients
Dr. Lazarus raise me up

Comme je deviens

Vielle fille, à manquer
du courage d'aimer la mort!

loud old Pullman brilliant a push

on Liquor *le coeur*

lash out

nay, jettison
person woven of floral language

insensate suddenly
& weight of the jaw, mandible lip
first speech, hirsute sleep but inside a pistil a stamen

someone saved her *madre* the consul

violence toward him

I demurred I stammer

advice
salute
say say a crime

said an hallucination
A dandelion spoke to me

it's certain
of mystery its grimaces

Che che che chivalry

chevre of lassitude

cash

hmmm delirium

phantom hyperion

in the hibarium

Person woven of laughter

fabric stitches together   seamless and seam-full

tropical trope in your diamond mind, voice's daughter

tesserae your incremental transmigratory realm

many figments are you?

stitch   stitch

a ceiling
a good children

but I can't pay anymore, sorry

good children, food for the good children

moreover I can't can't pay pay any more more more

it's a sash a ceiling above the celestial universe
and I can't can't pay pay any more

it's a cruelty

it's a really cruel cruelty

like you are not tested first
and more of a slash of a ceiling
on the other side throw a grimace   melts a rebus
chi   ta   cru cru   a real ti appearance of the rebus

it's a cure for cruelty

& in poor poverty

& in poor, poor poverty
and what you did or did not do

person woven of deeds doing and undoing cruelty

alchemy overdone seems always

as a verb

dune morphs to dojo vanity, a landscape

passage I do myself because
I am best at it

stars like Church Latin, you know en espanol

rising to intone the bounce of your vision percolating
high above the planet

looked down and saw

Person woven of small bouncing cars
Person woven of hand implements

Person woven of looking into one's hands

pins and sutras of attention or greed that would feed or
    starve the earth

and as she said that, the women next to her texting was missing
the yellow curtain of the ballet and as she said that
the red velvet of the interior, diamond clusters of the interior
the entrance of the conductor and his bow missed too
as she said that and turn it off turn it all off and
you ought look up, as she said that the seas parted…

Person woven into the Theatre of the Cambrian
sounds like it is that a Person woven is the sound of manioc
    not maniac

won't un-study for long

felicity of all religious *bêtes noires*

spec of other forms of control

nano regions

of transmigrating human dreams

how sad it seems we miss them

we see them moving and their tears
& are missing them coming now into our world

Person woven in the room, in the room to succor and sleep

and drink the vine

a line of men, a line of women and all between
a genderless spirit parity

and see one in the room so simple, open, you love him and
    feathered
love all the strangers tethered to the vine

a marred account
we are some of us occidental and there's no escape

you fail in all you fuel

because it's wrong wrong rung wrong
to sacrifice to artificial survival

Person coiled to strike back rung wrong

Iran syndrome

or pounce
Person lasting in extra parts to be diplomatic

part insect part machine keep missing one another
gleaming gleaning in the gloaming

Person appointed to measure how one walks and dips

external events

who tell? who believe? our frame!
entwined helix?

travel as explosions

future scene kind of lightly exists

stagger or faint on it

Go rising Not yet. Lost

then biosphere principle perpetuates the room and the
doorway and all about you a bother, a gossip off the page

parody of history

wasn't so much a scheme

wasn't so much a plan in a bubble as in hint of rumor

as if we are Person woven into a system where higher orders
are installed we can't even understand error or essence
   who to report to

Person woven of confusion

Person woven of fear

fumes

like a brat

canticles over in a hard night

done, the nuns, sing a matins sung, done done done

& speak of magnificent city heavenly city, *laudatio*

all the trees imploring and concrete imploring
O heavy heavenly sky

& you want the celibates to take over some charge

of Person-Woven-of-Many-Feminine-Forms
such as the big bellied effigy, pig belly of nails
the sow's ear is open, to listen
to drive your suffering down

entertain and enter jagged sky
& really want to be wracked with new chaos
child child child child
the child is father of the mother

last resolveno rejoice on mother stiletto, lift lift

goes other way *resolverio civilatio* kinosis the daughter is
wedgely an vocable hush hush is mother to herself, an ancestor
is vocable inside but silent is body is panthera moving
too mercenary a one
rubber boots of old survival kit
not necessarily interested in our new Person world view was a
Person but off catastrophe living was was was she even a Person?

milk my boy
rhythm of milk
the complications of milk how it is derived from the animal
sweet calve in agony, mother mad its stolen milk milk milk

mother mad its stolen milk milk milk milk

a narrow gate we walk into our genetic code it

twined

which is why I recognize you
were there code wars before we cooled down our heels
    down here?

did we win?

Person woven of all the others down here, and winning?

whoa

shrine a kind of jazz libation

Steve Lacy at the helm in "Materioso"

I went in my vision to visit the dead saxophone

my very own dead

in the list of daily duty so that loss is not lost

send down the mellow men to rock the inner coil
trembling is a future
when you lose your horn

when you lose a note
when you can't finish what you start

an A agent, a far gone forest argent ardent messenger
& way off his track but here arriving

money see money does fall from this body
small rupees, coins of old orient

but music pulls you back, his riff

red tassels with plums that are red and dark
Mohammed dawn

orange sunset and swirls of the stalking jaguar

multiple layers of cloth in weaving its process
body bound at vivid vivant waiting

Person woven like a shroud

but the ghosts are free!

Person woven of jazz guy tesserae

Taita guardian coming to me

prince of the vine

Taita in smoke and Taita smoking

bounce and a bounce, a bounce between tobacco worlds

serotonin   dopamine bounce

comes in from the left side *whuzzzzzsssssshhhhhhhhist awhoo awhoo*

syllables comes in from the right *za za za*

Person woven of sharp pinnacle of light above *a za za*
zig zag form of mental talk, maze protects from below

message? message?

Person woven of deeper sound singing and moving consistency
    to the sightings

order of our letters changes that's all!
all species and plant to human DNA

planet wired inextricably *za za awhoo*

body goes deeper into the earth

could be getting that close

I thought my heart would burst

I thought my gut would burst
bursting as a kind of firework
burst as a joy to see life crest
and you, supplicant, on that first crest
the fold of a robe
inner core burst
see first wave of my breath crest
  first word, first-come-serve heart
see feather that came for you
see claw that came for you

little earring that sounded your name
first heartbreak where you err on the path
a scald as bard as sleeping beauty
gone for countless eons until poetry blink you awake
a slant that burst, cut into your heart
an inscription on the turtle's belly
the bone divination that caught you on this life's wheel
slim chance this lifetime you could crest the wave
shake the rattle, honor the dead, the crucified hybriditic ones
precursors with their thought-string, cross-bows, boxes of dice
literal in the salt sea literal that you might be tested
in a slice of life to be their scribe, for the serial ones
those who come at night to send out seminal seed
and toward a crescent moon send those blessings
yet to be born, crops that will feed, healing balm that will succor
afflictions that will abate, put away your scriptures of doom
crepuscular time calling you between cracks of your vision

precarious to breathe in this world this time of cosmic night

Vision: coda strains in excess

Is anything central? Can you strive? Can you cure? Are you votive identity? The baby jaguar is blind at first. What are your roots and what are your severances and what do they constitute of imagination? Do you stalk can you heal will you climb. What is the link to the link of the trance of the trace of your heat-coil. Now you are quick, soon you will be dead. Ancestor! If roots are rural and you are on the ground barefoot, or if they are urban and you bend inwardly (your concrete sepulcher) will that help with the ground turning underneath your feet in jungle metaphor? And if the scene changes and suddenly abruptly something is riven— imploding rhythm—from you—then what? A new planet? What is being relational when you hardly know the kinetics of your own chemistry. And where you are from but you know goes back, back with all the other visitors who crowd your head. What will support mind in the longest sweetest deepest quivering night you live and notate within, and how will you move to caution others: be still, be very still…it's dawn in the adventure, space and time.

Vision: what men might be "being"

Men might be in the new frequencies being in the new forgiveness just equal in space being time continuum for adventure mission. Men miss out in the mission in the fission if not listening. To crack the code. If not listening then forcing their fiction. Might be aquatic or might say "pesky" and blue and rooted, what are the roots a down a hey ho down a down a derry derry down through earth. Be my pesky a down through the earth. They might be being male in studying topsoil better. Be being. And ground weird ire in better stargazing. Rooted to the light that never quite reaches, that already arrives, and stands, a body, some male body. in the doorway of duo paralysis. Paroxism. Metabolism of the grounded ones, but that never fixed because it is always moving, earth under our outside feet, wracked and aged from walking on earth bare footed. And what are the inside footsteps up and down the spine of your drum. I ask.

Perpetrator gone down, dust dust, not plunderer gone down dust dust not strategizing dust dust. But listen and absorb what is around you, the Male.

If you were a male of a particular order you could wear bird feathers. I would help you tie them on. I would help you with your accoutrements. I would hand you the accoutrements at the proper intervals of accoutrement-necessity. And then you are finally beautiful! I would give your voice a lilt and a rise. I would bounce with your song.

You could enter the realm of the guardians. We pay debts in parcels of light. It is a good idea.

Vision: where women have been woven is discerning
    riddle
adjacent to…her tongue
                  an oud, a harp, a mandolin

    a good idea

Vision : drink the gender line

cross lines you cross in lines and
    they be ever
best ever best you sound the lines cross of the
    gender line
    (yes yes go
cross the gender line down in muddy nothing in
 muddy something to sound
    (sound the
lines)
in mud twig mold realm for you
    inherit the earth
and the earth inherit you
lines pull you down
dram drum across a dress of twig and mud
kundry mouth kundry body ancient of drams
of Wolfram of Parzifal
loathly damsel hag offers the hero drink from
her golden german cup

drink drink the elixirs of knowledge
   your vision crossing dress kundry
of the poet-men hamper and thwart
 push through *yugas*
as said poet-men said a core in
   mud twig effigy
dress up childish power this way and
what would be like kundry
   (what would be like be like be like
a kundry doll,
 little obstacle)
as ancestors wide open in the earth,
   and you a kundry being
with obsession to right the male in me
   in effigy

did Whitman arrive to me. "me"
a woodswoman?
did he tell me "rive it thru, rive it thru"
he did, he did
did he give me power?
he did, he did

it was my own he saw he seered

Vision: Sister Susan

sister susan, come out now

sister susan come out now
with your bells on sister susan with your bells
and glimmer
come out, come out now
it's time it's time, sister susan
with your bells and glimmer

sister susan sister susan
with your glimmer and bells

Vision: Tesserae and Kundry

tesserae an interruption
tesserae an interrogation
all incentive tesserae to the fragments you inhabit
the broken body colors
the reconstituted machinations
panticks of strive-no-more
and stress of the past go down
    disintegrate
shards of stained glass of
strange shiny beetles devining

that carry crystals on
   the long march home
fractured blue glass and the
moons of a forgotten
     planet peek out
from a curtain in the sky
    curtain unfolded
unfolded in the brain
blue light   look up *heh heh*
     look in

Vision: to oscillate with my Ginsberg my Burroughs

is a wave
is a component
 signal
is
 frequency

oscillate
     my untrained ear in training
      steal their lines
       recombine our fire

Cepheid variable star....

as below so above

part of this world?

with Burroughs yage with Ginsberg yage I sang
a lump little fellow and to the curandero sang and sang

maestro jungle outskirts Pucallpa behind the gaswork field

talks a lot the power the curing cooks the universe together curing

talks a lot the drink the hold-it-together drinking

nite drinking session power curing strains the broth

hut an outskirt sincere in drug scape Ramon came over to hut

crooning a blowing a fresh batch & blowing cigarette and
    pipe smoke

over the cupmouth I rose

and Ramon came forth an old crooner

shooting star—Aerolito!

full moon I served up first breaking over the cupmouth

cavemouth runs over

whole fucking Cosmos broke loose around me

mosquitos, vomiting, silly to make this a note puff of smoke,
   mere death

and real death, real death, real death

all covered with snake like a Snake Seraph
colored serpents in aureole all around my body

and circling to love and include

a snake vomits the universe whoever she be

Jivaro with headdress with fangs vomiting up the Murder of
   the Universe

death to come death to come a mother to the universe

spectral animals all the other drinkers in the night in the awful
   solitude of the universe

went back and lay down, my woman inside

bastante, curandero!

heart rayed with spectral presences was what I got

all suffering transfiguration who believe and summon here

as there was the great stake the great stalk of Life and Death

expecting god knows what future snakes and obsoleth

being Natural, in abeyance, and neutered

skulking a beard on a pallet on a porch rolling back and forth

reproduction of the last physical move, coiling
great Being arriving approaching like a big wet vagina

in black hole of God nose

over the cupmouth I rose, ancestor

stronger and stronger in language

a being lay back on her back, jaguar spine

how strong you are she said in language

image: image how strong the colors of words

hammock and mosquito net for holding power in and away

35 *soles* about $1.50 for services

peer into a mystery, its cost

all creation present to weave itself back with out

colored snakes all real time, coiling

mild and simple for asking to be present

will you stand in or up for me in blue in green in yellow

of our movie only image I threw myself upon

so real I so real real phantom woven

witness the recovery of darkness to light

and not born yet her totem animal to be woven
days old slightly fermented, drink drink

what I thought was Great Mind was......false?

I felt somewhat like the eye is imaginary
predator jaguar was the crashing jaguar hissing *awhoo*

and the eye was seeing through itself a woman–poet

"singing mysterious things" that was our fate in the dawn house

and humming *b'alam, b'alam*

leave my body to be found in the luminous morning

Yage
Boulder, September
Gloucester, October
Captiva, April
2013

NOTES :

Kundry is an old crone, an earth goddess, but on the other side of the mountain in the magic garden of the sorcerer Klingsor (in Wagner's *Parsifal*), she is a beautiful maiden.

3-brane world refers to theories in particle physics and cosmology related to string theory, super-string theory and M-theory where branes are like thin slices of bread. Put them together and you have the multiverse.